E.J. Makes Good Choices

Story by Sandi Hannigan
Illustrations by Kris Westbeld

Ernest J. Swalm was a person who made some very
important choices in his life. Some of the choices
were easy to make. But some of them were
very difficult choices. He often had
to make very hard decisions.

Ernest was born in the year 1897. When he was a young boy, his friends nicknamed him E.J. E.J. had a great sense of humor; he liked to tell jokes and make his friends laugh.

E.J. was born and raised in Duntroon, Ontario, Canada. He lived on a farm with his dad, his mother, and his younger sister, Pearl. There was always plenty of work to do on the farm.

E.J.'s pet was a large, strong dog named Goliath, who followed E.J. as he did his chores on the farm. "Come on, Goliath," E.J. would call, and Goliath would run along beside E.J. wherever he went.

Autumn was the busiest time of the year on the farm. "E.J.," called his dad, "I need your help. There are plenty of juicy, ripe apples to pick and pack for market."

E.J.'s dad had only one arm and depended greatly on E.J.'s help. His dad reminded him, "Always remember to pack the same good quality apples on the bottom of the basket as you do on the top."

As a young boy, E.J. learned
to be honest helping his father sell
apples. He knew it was wrong
to hide poor apples on the bottom
of the baskets. People appreciated
E.J.'s honesty in packing apples.

E.J. was a boy who spent a lot of time just thinking about things. "I wonder where God lives?" he thought as he worked around the farm. "I wonder if God likes to climb apple trees?" he thought as he picked apples. "I wonder if God has a pet?" he thought as he played with Goliath. E.J. liked the outdoors and he felt close to God when he was in the orchard.

As a child, E.J. attended the Brethren in Christ Church. He enjoyed listening to the preachers and others speak.

He knew many Bible stories, and his favorite one was the story of the Good Samaritan. E.J. liked the story because of the kindness and compassion of the Good Samaritan.

When E.J. was twelve years old, he chose to become a follower of Jesus Christ. "I want to live like Jesus lived. I want to choose God's ways. I want to treat others with respect and love," said E.J.

This was the most important choice E.J. ever made. This decision made a difference in the way he thought and lived his life. He learned to think about how his actions affected other people.

When E.J. was a teenager, he said to his parents, "I would like to be baptized as a follower of Jesus." He was baptized in a river with twelve friends from his youth group. They also became members of the Brethren in Christ Church.

E.J. and his friends enjoyed
doing things together, like playing baseball
in the summer and hockey in the winter.

As a follower of Christ, E.J. said,
"I believe everyone's life is valuable and precious.
I could never fight or kill anyone."
Sometimes he wondered what it would be like if there
would be a war. He wondered what he would do.

In 1914, World War I began far away in
Europe. By then, E.J. was a young man.
He got a letter saying, "You must
become a soldier and go to war."
But E.J. knew he could not
fight and kill anyone.

An army official tried very hard to make E.J. change his mind and become a soldier. "Ernest John Swalm," the army officer said, using E.J.'s full name, "you are a coward and disgraceful. If you do not fight, you will be put in chains, taken overseas, and killed by the enemy."

But E.J. would not change his mind. He was not afraid of the official's threat. "I believe so strongly in peace and non-violence," E.J. said, "that I am willing to risk my life for my beliefs. I will not fight. I will not go to war. I will not kill."

Sometime later, E.J. heard someone
knock on his door. When he opened the door,
he received a paper ordering him to go to war.
The paper said: "Report immediately to the
Army barracks in Hamilton, Ontario, Canada."

Again, E.J. knew he could not go to war.
When E.J. reported to the barracks, he said boldly,
"I'm a conscientious objector. I will not fight.
I will not kill. I will not go to war."
"Forget it!" they said.
"When we are through with you, you'll change your mind about being a C.O."
("C.O." is what persons were called who were conscientiously opposed to joining the military.)

E.J. did not change his mind about being a conscientious objector in spite of their threat. He remained true to his words and to his commitment to being a peacemaker. E.J. was arrested and put in prison because he refused to go to war.

Going to prison was a high price to pay for his beliefs. But because he decided to do what he thought was right, E.J. was an example of courage to many men in the prison.

When E.J. returned home,
some people said, "E.J., you are
a coward because you did not go to war."

But others stood by him and commended him. "You are a courageous man, E.J. We respect you for the difficult choices you made. Many of the decisions you faced were not easy ones to make. But you made wise choices, E.J. You are a fine example to us."

After he was released from prison, he married his girlfriend, Maggie.

In my part of Canada, back country roads become muddy, with deep ruts made by cars and trucks. Once your car gets into one of those ruts, it's very hard to get out of it. That's the way life is — choose your "rut" very carefully, because you'll be in it a long time!

He also became a very good preacher. Everyone listened carefully to his stories and many people who heard him came to believe in God.

E.J. was also highly respected by many people in Mennonite and Brethren in Christ churches.

Because he made good decisions, he was given many opportunities to serve as a leader in the church.

Another war began in Europe in 1939.

"How shall we approach the government?"

"It might be best if we would work together to present our beliefs about Christians not participating in war."

The next year, he invited people from Mennonite, Brethren in Christ, Church of the Brethren, and Friends churches. Together they organized a group called "The Conference of Historic Peace Churches."

E.J. worked hard to make suggestions for peace to the government. He was respected by the Prime Minister. He had ideas of helpful service projects for people to do who did not want to go to war.
Instead of going to war, they would agree to do community work and service projects.

Many of the conscientious objectors were sent to the Montreal River, a very rugged and remote part of Canada. They were building a highway to stretch across Canada. Others were sent further west in Canada to fight forest fires. Still others went to these burned areas to plant trees.

E.J. received an important assignment.
"E.J., your assignment is to be a minister to
the C.O.'s who are working near the Montreal River."
E.J. responded, "I will go,
even though it means
leaving my family
and friends."

As a minister, E.J. traveled many miles to visit
conscientious objector camps and hospital units.
He encouraged the C.O.'s. "Be true to your peace
beliefs and to God, my friends," he said.

Although the C.O.'s were from different churches, they discovered they had much in common. They all believed that violence was wrong and that everyone's life was precious.

E.J. said, "These men are some of God's choice servants!"

Many years passed, and E.J. served the church as a pastor and a leader. He died in August 1991, at the age of 94. As an old man, he was thinking about his life and the many choices he made. E.J. said, "Being a Christian is a lifetime job. There are difficult choices to make, like whether or not to join the army. God always gives us the courage to do what is right and to make wise choices. By the grace of God we must take our stand!"

MORE ABOUT E. J. SWALM

Ernest John Swalm was born Jan. 25, 1897, near Duntroon, Ont. He was the son of Bishop Isaac and Mary Alice Swalm.

In his memoirs, *My Beloved Brethren*, published in 1969, he wrote, "From infancy, church attendance was a regular part of my life. With gratitude I recall growing up in the spiritual and social atmosphere of our home congregation, now known as the Stayner Church. Here I was converted. In this church I was received into membership. Here I received my first communion. In this sanctuary I was ordained to the ministry and later to the office of bishop. Here I gave pastoral leadership for nearly thirty years."

In 1918, during World War I, the Canadian government began conscripting every man from 20 to 23. The first member of the Canadian Brethren in Christ Church to be drafted was Ernest Swalm, then 21. Information about the new conscription policies was limited and confusing; it was not clear whether previous provisions for exempting Conscientious Objectors were still in effect.

Appearing at the military base only a week after getting his notice, E.J. repeated his decision to stand by his nonresistant beliefs. The officers used flattery, ridicule, and intimidation, trying to change his mind. When ordered to put on a uniform, E.J. courteously refused. Instead, he offered to serve in any kind of medical or relief work if he could do so as a non-uniformed civilian. Finally, and without any resistance on his part, he was stripped of his civilian clothes, dressed in army fatigues, court-martialed, and sentenced to ten years of hard labor in prison.

After he was in prison four weeks, the government recognized the exemption privileges it had granted in the past for members of nonresistant churches. So E.J. was released on parole. Four months later, the war ended.

In 1920, E.J. married Maggie Steckley. They had three daughters (Lela, Jean, and Mildred) and one son (Ray). Although he lived all of his life on the family farm, he had a ministry that spanned North America. In addition to pastoring the Stayner congregation for many years, he served as a bishop in the Canadian Brethren in Christ Church from 1929 to 1967. He traveled across Canada and the United States as an evangelist, conducting 354 revival meetings. And he provided leadership to a number of interdenominational organizations, such as the Ontario Conference of Historic Peace Churches, the Presidium of the Mennonite World Conference, the Canadian Bible Society, and the Evangelical Fellowship of Canada.

E.J. Swalm (far left) and his sister Pearl (far right) with friends on his parent's farm in Ontario. This picture was taken in 1908, when E.J. was 11 years old.